CONSIDER THE ROOSTER

OLIVER BAEZ BENDORF

CONSIDER THE ROOSTER

NIGHTBOAT BOOKS

NEW YORK

Copyright © 2024 by Oliver Baez Bendorf

Printed in Lithuania

ISBN: 978-1-643-62238-5

Cover design and typesetting by Kit Schluter
Typeset in University Roman and Goudy Old Style

Cataloging-in-publication data is available
from the Library of Congress

Nightboat Books
New York
www.nightboat.com

What is—"Paradise"—
Who live there—

—EMILY DICKINSON, #215

each one an active
displacement in perspective;
each screaming, "This is where I live!"

—ELIZABETH BISHOP, "Roosters"

When the rooster jumps up on the windowsill
and spreads his red-gold wings,
I wake, thinking it is the sun

—AI, "Cuba, 1962"

CONTENTS

I just chose my place

It is technically my ethic to share.

—DR. KIM TALLBEAR

COLONY COLLAPSE

begins without shelter in a storm. what
I have to do next. I sleep best
at anyone else's house. I like the ones that bees
like. I think madness is colonization. I know
grace is how I'm still alive. shock
of blue jay on an oxidized fence. I try
to make a religious exception. don't die
of perfectionism. heave along the goldenrod—begin
to live more together. I try to unravel spanish

ways of knowing, for example, crown on my head

in an empty field . . . we plant
lavender and let it grow
bushy for the bees. sexy how they feed on blooms.

pleasure, time, money, faith, yucca, evil, each
one multiplies—we never eat alone. come
over, I will be a confidential lover
to each
one of you. private things, private thoughts. we bake
breadcrumbs into royal
jelly. I love with every hand, horse, water, wind. if you wonder
where to rear the young, if you too fall
feverish after that communal feeling. swear to god
when I'm
dead I'll spend years waiting for the living
to call, offer wine and dance. I need
everyone I love. I'm too tired.

time to feed our missing before they come
gone. third eye is a gloryhole. door's open.   soup's on.

BECOMING PARTICULATE

When a voice met the resonant frequency of the object,
when the song crashed into glass as invisible waves,
at last I began to vibrate. Finally! I exploded like a garage
window the year the rooster sang. What was it that rattled
me so astrologically? Or does it matter only
that I was rattled, propelled from my brittle bunker
into a new position, compromised now by such beauty
as mist caressing a mountain, or how heavy
the satchel of ashes lands against my ribcage? I pray
my recollection of the neighbor dissolves into nothing
when we leave this town, that however much the song
I love rattled him too, that he forgets me entirely
for he exploded in a different way. Something
about my mother is I learned to dry plastic baggies
upside down. Though I'd never plant grass in a place
I'm meant to stay, I try to reach every last seed
with my mouth now the promise of leaving
glows the horizon. Learning to speak the language of mums,
I ask myself how the fear of small
particles affects my everyday experience. Today I give
thanks for the way, in pestilence, living has gone on.
I remember Dilly by her bones, now pulverized, like
dust of the dead, in whose light we still read our future.

ALL I HAVE IS THE WOODS INSIDE MY HEAD

Minerva, calm me down. I am trying
to remember the way the deer always
emerged every time I thought of them.
And how bones would surface in the dirt
at the marsh. I'm sniffing pinecones
back to the forest floor. Rubbing
fingers together to make moss. Smoking

    toward the orchard where I could
    never find the owl in the rotting
    tree. What kind of tree? I can't
    remember! Years pass. I'm at my desk
    doing a hormone shot with my
    cam off, and trying to remember,
    when someone in the webinar

        on trans femme aesthetics says
        they don't believe anything's
        innate. I laugh (on mute), I too
        have been tossing nurture~nature
        in my mind, but who hasn't? Now what
        god threw up this unforgettable
        sunset tonight? I step out

            to the deck in my trans masc robe
            because in the end, no one will
            remember. All that I've named
            has a life outside of me. On
            certain days, when the humidity
            is just right, I remember everything.
            I regret nothing. Birch tree.

IMPERVIOUS

Someone stops over unannounced like the old days,
so I pop open that bottle of Sancerre I've been saving.
Talk turns to carp that reached the roadway
after Thursday's three inches of rain, how some said
invasive, let them die, others said *naturalized*,
let them live, someone asked for a net and
                                        others said
they'd catch them with their hands. I could
never do what the raccoon does, tossing
pink petals, or could I? We go to the club that
turns gay only on Saturday nights. In the morning,
I'm still gay, thank god. But the rain, it's returning.

WHAT IS A FIELD

is it a network for stars to enjoy

how about a box for answers tube of empire   interface

with verdant properties   discrete sensory invitations

is it a complete cloud system   full of muscle   prairie password

could a field

be a fertile facial   my secret

   seasoning wet

seed of another lonely moon?   did the forest   almost   watch?

WHO PROFITS FROM THIS FEELING

coffee filters, clay, red string, mist machine, tempera paint, binoculars, goat's wool

The rainbow is a collection of rays with particular directions, and gender is like a cone of light opening outward. I wanted to show the way some people are so obsessed with revealing gender that it becomes a kind of constriction on an otherwise open flow of solar rays. Creating a so-called bottle-neck through which every other issue must pass. Each person has their own cone and sees their very own rainbow. It does not otherwise exist and it is not located at any particular point in space. If you have accumulated something like shame, you are invited to practice every day getting rid of it. You could walk it to the edge of your body and out the door and down the street over and over and over again. However many times it takes. Return to sender. The rainbow angle is the angle of minimum deviation. Who benefits from this distraction? Particulates from wildfire make their way into every new experience.

I WANT BIODEGRADABLE SEX

polypropylene, moss, human hair, pine needles, cardboard, sheepskin condoms, coffee grounds

This sculpture reveals the demand my transition has created for the plastics industry over time. By melting plastic syringes into a compressed form, I hope to create an anticlimax by showing all at once the slow accumulation of material. When you observe me and then the sculpture, is the volume of plastic more or less than what you would expect? Do you agree strongly, agree, neither agree nor disagree, disagree, or strongly disagree that certain plastics should remain single-use? By incorporating an assortment of organic elements, I wanted to create a sense of grief out of the cognitive dissonance. Plastikos, to form or mold, an art long before plastics were invented. Trans is a way of arranging the world through change, but plastic is durable, meaning it never goes away. Very light, gets blown along in gentle winds. It gets washed by rain into sewers, streams, rivers, and finally oceans. It burns forever in landfills, a campfire around which we tell scary stories. It is pleasurable at times when a container fulfills the functions for which it has been designed. I hope to return to earth a little bit more every day, until I'm finally you again.

EVERYONE WANTS SOME OF MY PRAIRIE

Breath, unbound from desire for it.
Pollen across a field. Me
going quiet for it like
owls do, the only sound at all their quiet nothing—
      how heavy it is. Everyone wants a ride in my combine.
The streets
are numerals and "he"
      is taking place in a future he has.
The day imparts several
visual patterns which I understand as likeness
until someone says "correspondences." I like
the part where I look up and the stars

don't look back at me and
the coyotes don't howl back and years
of dark shapes in the corners of the field come back like
      wind does, like
breath that has blown through everyone.

DREAM STRUCTURE

We were circling
up for something and   I just—

I JUST CHOSE MY PLACE AND LET THE CIRCLE FORM AROUND ME

behold   *the Lord*   a neutron star *had*   been "missing" for thirty-two years

visible light faded

                                                 gradually over 500 days, then

astrophysicists *announced*   they had seen a hot, bright

blob in the core

of Supernova 1987A

wouldn't it feel pleasant to be   *more and more* together like a neutron star

clearly a brotherhood since we're all exploding anyway? Might as well hedge

that spinning rank   *it was*   an "agent of change"   I stood there squinting

into the heavens thinking if "star" can also be "dust cloud" or "nebula"

or "black hole" then surely gender is far stranger than we've imagined

and much more beautiful, unfurling over decades, a phenomenon.

Exploded from a corn field—that's me. Will you join this velvet burst?

Even the Lord wants it. *His* will   was written down for everyone

to read and he left something for everyone. The *intention* of the cedar

wood *and* hyssop branch and scarlet yarn is to let it be known that it feels good to dwell in unity and *pleasure*. If I'm someday judged

on group projects alone, pray for me, *nay*, pray for you! But I wonder

will wealth be measured by what I gave away? I am interested in the gods,

their names, powers, and most of all what they gave up for power. *Holy*

lightning bolts *will* not come from my hand, but I too am unfolding, changing.

An old Amana book I read, *that* one with the cloth orange cover, says

before there was anything else, the communal kitchens along the river valley,

the calico, the salsify, before any barn or house was built, before the mill fire,

before *everything* that had to do with industry, there was the Community

of True Inspiration—the church, the faith, the religion—most of all.

The year I was born, a supernova exploded in "our" skies. I was thirty-two when

dust settled to finally reveal its thick, luminescent core. I didn't even know.

I *should* keep the faith. So I'm here. *Be* a cloud with me   remember

the believers   by how they plant their dead in the ground   absolute

order of expiry   identical stone monuments bearing names *and* years

measuring lifespan

by number of orbits taken

around an already dying

star!

I'm coming back to me now, yet I *remain in common.*

Come get your eggs: laid from the elements of dead stars!

transition is always a relief

Destination means death to me. If I could figure out a way to remain forever in transition [...] I could remain in a state of perpetual freedom.

—DAVID WOJNAROWICZ

BOREAL

Boreal was the word for what
we wanted from each other—thinking
it meant trees. Dream unfolds inside
heavy wooden frame. Fresh red
deer to the side of the service road.
Not a cold snap, but a morning
in a pine forest, great warm giver
of the sky tilting heads. Brown
bears burning fear back
into awe. No treasur-
y. I don't want to think
about money. I'll eat anything
and, later, dream of it. That's what
omnivorous means. I'd straddle a log
if it reminded me, but I'd burn
an entire river to forget.

T4T

FOR ALEX

And I think he must be drunk, from the sweet way he.
Brother. I think about his XX all the time. It's like a joke,
That we'll start dreaming of men once we. My favorite
Version is the one where we. We ate citrus on river rock
While others swam out. Stern lady cop found us out-of-
Towners naked. Our clothes scattered around pine root.
Dampened for days. But he. Inclination surges
Through window screen—that wind, you'd think
We'd found ourselves in beach town.
If I had the chance, I'd go right to the root of him.
Shouldn't I out of anyone feel it with my main medium.
I think there's something happy and right about us mating.
That night how you. Chest flying. Tonight my house creaks.
Somewhere swings open a gate we all know we all want.

RAM'S HEAD WHITE HOLLYHOCK AND LITTLE HILLS

O'Keeffe said the bone was about form, not death.
The shape the skull made floating in that blustery sky.

Skull built like a sturdy wooden box, like a weapon.
Wherever you lay the ram's head, you will create

soft red hills underneath. You will never forget
the light. It frolics all day long. The horns twist upward

into each corner. Uncoiled at the end of a long day.
By someone close. A friend. The hollyhock appears

almost tucked behind the ram's ear. So the ram
wanted to know how it felt to adorn. To self-mark

with a bloom meaning there is something fertile here.
The ram could bear a lamb,

perhaps.
Could.

If he wanted to.
Would he bundle it over winter

or carry it prominently, like a hollyhock at the temple?

Remember
the little hills, which bloom and skull

will someday both become. The hills where each
drought is longer than the one before.

Once, in front of windows for the reconstructed
prairie to see, my uncle spun me by my ankles.

Corners of the room became a blur, a happy palimpsest.
I laughed and laughed
till the orbit shot a woozy arrow into my stomach—

crystals in the ear dislodged.
Nothing ever looked the same.

Dizziness defines the center.

WILL AND TESTAMENT

I want to be buried under timber and rock
like Caeneus was. I'll be immune to weapons,
even once they find original female, soft
in the wrong places, scarred. Leave me in
a woods somewhere quiet, let my ribs
rattle with the woodpecker's industry.
Let the heavens fade lilac to orange on
the longest night. I'll leave you candles.
May raccoons walk their spidery prints all
over the dirt, may berries sprout
magic. I leave you my pleasure and joy
for which I worked so hard. I wish you
lusty longing and rapt attention. Though
the twiggy lean-to off the trail is not my
property to transfer, I hope you find it.
I offer you my bright dumb
hopes for democracy. May your vote always
be counted. Your body was made
to shift shape. Seek to serve. Come visit me where
pines loop, tell me joy you're having. Tangible form. Isn't it amazing,
the golden needles dropped,
how they leave a pad
on the ground
for your tent. Grove
awaits. Already
abandoned
my body once—look what happened after.

ME AND ALL THAT IS UNSOLVED. ME AND THE FIRE

Dear tadpoles, I already hatched
So many of you. There at night
Do you know what to feel
With each other, do you see shadows
Flying overhead?
I'd just died when
The eaglet did—so like me, weeping over a webcam.
Get hungry and your name so soon.
To sleep some person yet.
Does it hurt to say we saw.
Can you tell us what we saw, was it.
Just some glorious raccoon in
Gelatinous debt. Didn't make
Tadpoles, we were always
So different.
I could be more patient
With all that is unsolved
In your heart. I forget
Your family dealt with fire
By going around it. Life is
So short. And loving
With patience so hard. Wind is so
                        Weird the way it
Touches me, ruffles my atmosphere. Not now, wind, can't you see I'm
Trying to notice humidity, temperature,
And other conditions I take for granted.

THE BEASTS HAVE BEEN TOO KIND

Season of see-through
deciduous, fallen
limbs lying

in repose. What's
unpassable
in snowfall is still

a simple leap. Please
watch your feet
on decomposing

leaves. Blueberry
light stretches
swollen fingers

between trunks. Din-
a brunch. Laundry
singes nasal

hairs, blocks
from any
basement.

All night,
lamplight

knocks
against
my window

from the top
of the ravine.
Though the beasts

have been
too kind, the Barred
Owl has been

asking: *Who*
cooks for you? Who
cooks for you

all? The terrible
moment when
one wants

to say everything.

GOD OF MEDICINE

Crito, we owe a cock to Asclepius. Please, don't forget to pay the debt.
                              —SOCRATES *(allegedly his last words)*

    So I returned to the room and held out my hand. I held
my hand out and she took it. And we descended
    that staircase. We walked down those stairs and out
      the front door. We passed through the front

    door and into the rest of my life. I brought
her up to speed on the decades.
 I decided

    finally to live and so we walked into my life.
      There is no room. There is only the house we build.

THE HAWK IS GONE, LONG LIVE THE HAWK

Blue isthmus opens overhead. Into a sudden, stunning brightness

casting glare
onto the page

where Telethusa prays to have Iphis expressed through another form.

OFFERINGS IPHIS PLEDGED AS A GIRL AND PAID AS A BOY

I called myself a man (which I think
I am) so I could talk about how good
the crying feels now I've learned to let it.
Some days it's as simple as the way
the clouds dry, a watercolor wash set
down against the great nothing, in colors
I choose not to name. I've feared my life
transpiring without me. Revelations
I've been too stubborn, or too afraid.
I missed two good friends' weddings,
caught in the silk of my own misery.
We pretend we don't need one another's
love on our skin. It's how little I laughed
some years. I love the ones I didn't know
were coming, lenient clovers. But I also
love the jonquils I waited for all winter,
each one an orange candle, another wish.
For all I've missed. For everything to come.
The way all feelings come and go, like rain,
which changes the very color of living things.

MICHIGAN

You all tell me, go and hide my tail between my legs.
I will no longer put up with this shit.
I have been beaten.
I have had my nose broken.
I have been thrown in jail.
I have lost my job.
I have lost my apartment.
For gay liberation, and you all treat me this way?
What the fuck's wrong with you all?
Think about that!

—SYLVIA RIVERA

daisy fleabane arrives early after winter onslaught of lake effect

snow melt becomes water that feeds wildflowers from the underside

becomes flood

comes family

a cellular structure for secrets

the year is 2020

everyone is sick and healing

not everyone

everyone is sick *or* healing

lives are precious or expendable

expelled, expressed, released, sighed

sloughed off to replicate in someone else's precious or expendable lungs

germination, occupation

months between vagus nerve and a memory of sociality

you might as well be in Michigan

I rolled into a pleasant peninsula seeking safe haven

and yes sometimes an invisible cloak fits over my house

caped children walk by carrying plastic pumpkins

I push grass ordinance to edges

a local construction of crime

legal height lowered

brace for tensions with neighbors

I mow a tiny strip around the meadow

the pollinator garden tickles the curb with liberated wildflowers

fleabane daisies such a startling puff of yellow

pink clover right over and dock

dead limbs rotting but controlled into compost

we will grow things here, "we are in this together"

I'll post a sign explaining

and pray no one calls

on the rooster

who rushes to elevation to greet the day

or warn of it

all day the same bugle meaning something only in his kingdom

which I happen to live in

I surround myself in brown

deck stains and elk and moose

of the Michigan flag

state whistle toad song

don't you know? sun cooks

the shame away

who else needs to survive

I am trying to answer one question

I measure miles from the arbitrary border

drive-through pharma for extra

vials of testosterone—controlled substance

Rx sees a criminal queer

scrutinizes ID then dispenses a paper bag folded closed and stapled which I toss

empty passenger seat sanitize my hands keep driving

fueled by fossils

north in Michigan what is a mortgage

is it a house of cards a debt meant never to be repaid

token of achievement in settlement's shadow

am I the last loser in Michigan still banking

on silence and pleasantries to protect me

strangers/neighbors power walk past my ragged lawn

their yards are dull and starve hummingbirds, monarchs, cardinals, and bees how is that more beautiful?

if I stay in line

if I keep my head down

if I work harder

et cetera

I have held my tail between my legs and sang "grateful"

I have been spit on for whose hand I held, harassed for the pants I wore, catcalled for existing

I have been slandered by the God Hates Fags family

I studied their church compound on Google Street View

and saw the Pride center painted in rainbow across the street

I can no longer be placated by the colorful advancement of rights

depressed: to push or pull down

no wonder

an old ordinance still on the books

bans fortune telling

another way I am a criminal here

between that and the forbidden meadow

and some other elements

and the privileges I am often permitted

I forgot to assemble, paid on time every month

did homophobia's work by playing "smear the queer"

Sylvia didn't DIE for me to hide my tail between my legs

so I untether from my respectable nest

holding the "x" in my hand like a rosary

and like a brick

I'm done being good!

spirit in flight

Well, I run around like a spirit in flight. Fearlessness is fearlessness.

—STEPHANIE LYNN NICKS

SPELL FOR BURNED BOOKS

Juniper branches
burned
become calcium.
Herb burns

into relief.
It destroys nothing.
Nazi
book burns

began with
third
gender history
plundered—

20,000 books
torched
in Opernplatz.
Paper into

ash, smoke,
water vapor.
Take your
eternal flames

of damnation
back.
We've become,
as we always

have, another
form entirely.

A DREAM ABOUT FALLING TIMBER

Tree trunk ran perpendicular
to trail and water, binding them.
Wind shivered through the lone
pine.
I've brought an empty bowl and a prayer.
"I need a good idea."

Inside the house, a dream about falling timber.
All along, some people cried and others were
                                        so excited.
        Earthy aroma of
                            —there's no other way
        to say this—dandelion. To know how.
I'm lost in the indeterminacy of our timeline.

WONDERLAND

Didn't I see them? Weren't
there three? Weaving a curved path
around the neighbor's tree? How can
it be that already their tracks
have become divots in fresh
snow untraceable from any
other footfall? I stood
in the picture window. I rushed out
in my socks. Leaving my own prints
where theirs eluded me. How should I be
both beautiful and strong? It was as if
the atmosphere had a pink
story. The atmosphere was pink
for a while as I walked back,
and heavy. Never look a deer
in the face. The whites of human
eyes give me away. Like a gift.
To a god. The whites of my eyes
give away that I am watching.
And when

should I run? And when to fight?
Look at me.
A deer always knows. I am listening
with everything I have for love
and danger.

FREQUENTLY THE WOODS ARE PINK

FOR HANK

When I was your age, I played in what I remember as an unending forest.
I knew the way in and the way out, but not the perimeter.
When it was time for dinner, I'd emerge with longing and relief.
I never thought to ask how flowers bloom.
Or how some buds emerge from almost any point along a twig.
Life passed forward as if by sheer proximity. By that and the intrepid carriers
Of pollen. It is through this magic that I can be an uncle to you.
And try to impart some of what's good in me.
I try to love myself as if I am some imperfectly shaped flower. No less miraculous
For being one of many. Somehow, many bad and good things happen
Even though it is possible that we, along with asters,
Are simply stardust trying to know itself again. For the sake of beauty
And change, which is also beautiful. Where you and I once
Lived, horticulturists cast predictions on when peak cherry bloom
Will come, for the benefit of tourists making plans, when people traveled.
I always felt that the delight of the prediction was mainly
That they could be wrong. That despite their algorithms, something
Could still elude the most exact approximation humans can buy.
By some surprising collusion of sun, rain, wind, temperature, and
Whether or not anyone dared to sing in the shadows. And we love
The blooms for that. For defying us with their own timeline. Feels good
To long for them before they open up, and recollect their fragrance later.
Today, I am thirty-three years old. You are seven. Together, we
Are at the top of some hill, and I am trying to leave you something.
To love yourself as though most of the elements in your body
Have passed through several supernovas, which they have.
Stardust, which is how I am your uncle. Asters in a field.
Each one a friend to keep close. I am still learning who my god is,

Laid wreaths at many right and wrong altars.
How is it that when Astraea wept, her tears became starflowers?
They sprang up from the ground below where she felt sorry.
Everyone has a different reason why. Mortals stranded in a flood,
Or not enough stars in the sky. Can you imagine? Wanting
Even more stars in the sky? It's like wanting more Christmas
Than the amount of Christmas there already is. My grandmother
Wanted more Christmas. She and my grandfather traveled
To Europe for more Christmas to bring back to Iowa:
Nutcrackers, ornaments, nativity scenes, and candle pyramids.
Opened a shop next to their red brick house, set back a ways.
What I remember most is the tinsel and ribbon. Short scraps
In every color, handed out to me and my sister along with lemon
Drops. And I canceled my subscription to Ancestry.com, so instead I am writing
You about the woods, which are pink, and brown, and powerful.

Rx

*In my new healing, I learned
that we are all sick.*
—WILLIE PERDOMO

Can poetry keep my mosquito
population down, or will I need
to hang a bat-house? Can a poem
ensure my right to non-discrimination
as I age? Must I trade my tongue for shelter?
Who is responsible
for hope? Is anyone in charge of freedom?
Can a poem hurry the half-life

of insecticides?
Trying to make the first disaster better,
we refuse. We
want reduced. We have prescriptions.
Can you sing? Pray? Bang a pot in the street
until you remember? If you're reading this,
illuminate a candle in your window tonight. I love you.

NEBRASKA

I had almost forgotten about fields of hay bales

And the way the fog sits low over the ground hands trying to warm themselves over heat

I forgot how small coyotes look when lying dead on the side of the road RIP

If you've heard them howl once at night, you hear them every night for the rest of your life or I do anyway I forgot

How specific the color red is in October everyone pictures

Orange this month but for me it's red ritual red rosebud red apple red

My blood still inside me red because I'm all about living these days I cover my face

To go inside a gas station brick red rainbow red Walter's comb the day we left him and some of the hens in Schoolcraft I had almost forgotten

How this pattern lives inside me bales staggered in an open field to dry I hope

The spirits of my ancestors follow me west on 80 Gennarena Cristina Emmaline Julius I had almost forgotten

The way a single tree looks in an open field

Past the exit for the pony express I thought

The fog would've lifted by now burned off wherever it goes

Left Michigan without any fanfare no parties still a pandemic

For six days the neighbors watched us pack the truck arrange and rearrange belongings I'm tired

Of watching them watch us those neighbors which is one reason why I'm glad we're leaving

Should reach Olympia in a few days.

SUNSHINE LEATHER REVIVAL

The weekend basketball reenters my life
I dream I'm trying to give a presentation

printed on orange wedges. Little faces
of bright clementines, looking for language
where there should not be any, maybe only

sound of hands dribbling a god around
a painted floor. A crowd cheers and claps
as they dunk comet into a net mounted

from the sky. Someone wears the mask
of the mascot, and fans
break into chants and gesture,

nachos!, and oh, the band . . . the brass . . .
trombone exiting the arena bangs its upper horn
first left, then right, against metal doors,

then bursting out into that bluebird sky,
which had melted the snow—or was that the heat
emanating from the bright orange ball,

sphere of leather being thrown around?
Venus and Jupiter big in the starry night.

MATTERS OF ECOLOGY

Four legs made the sky turn a pink you wouldn't
believe. Everything converged in a single field,
which was every field my eyes laid upon while they

had visions of merriment my ears strained to hear.
The ridge hid the animal from thoughts of passing
cars. Something odd about the year thirty-five
came to rest at the pull-off where the almost remaining

raccoon blended blissfully into landscape,
save for the sole expressive punctuation
marking where it lay: a hawk. The angle
facing the road was the good side, still intact.

Look what faced the field, though. A red
interior that weeks later I woke from a dream trying
to remember and trying to forget.

Each morning the rise of daylight faces
the other side of the house, and still I cannot sleep.
What form has become of this love? As what shape

will these years return?

So that the two in the car could not, I looked. Or
I looked because they wouldn't. Maybe none of this
matters. What matters is we left it there and drove

along, so that the hawk could return, because sometimes
it's time to leave, and what seems inevitable sometimes
is, no matter whether or not you stay to watch.

EVERYTHING ALL AT ONCE

right now,
someone is having sex and someone
is dying and someone is trying to find
a lid so they can, before bed, put away
the soup and someone is dreaming
of that made meadow and someone
is gazing through a hospital window
to a faraway peak
and someone can't decide what
to watch so they remain

on the menu screen for company
and someone wants to call but
can't and someone wants to answer
but won't and someone is studying
to become a moth scientist and someone
is dizzy and doesn't know why
and someone is, after work, practicing
the vocal techniques of opera
and someone receives
a phone call saying listen it's my

neighbor I told you about the singing one can you
hear it and someone
is clutching the heavy still warm hand
of a lover and someone is digging
a hole and someone is waxing
their back and someone
is remembering a poem permitting
bits and pieces to return
and someone
would do almost anything to forget

EXPANDING THE ENCOUNTER

I would have to go back to the seeds
that grew the dandelions which I crossed
the street to pluck
upon returning
to juvenile rabbit dead in the middle
of the footpath bugs now feeding
hide freckled with holes and fluxing
insect lines following their nose
probably.
—to when the road
was built, when its name
was changed. To fur-flecked
coyote scat that began to appear

after campus emptied. I would have to
return to the fox beckoning from switchbacks
that melted into pine grove. I would need
to reverse
into night, possibly, or very
early morning. I would want to know

the creatures feeding on it, where will
they go, what will this become.
I would have to acknowledge
that the rabbit died before

I got there and will continue
dying longer after I walk
these few blocks home,
under moon, to sit

in my apartment and write.
Count them: five yellow flowers
laid across
the rabbit's ribcage, varying

my repetition of staying in the middle
of the path, because the rabbit
was dying there, had already gone.
I offered it all I had, someone else's poem:

You're sitting here with us, but
you're also out walking in a field at dawn.

WHAT THE DEAD CAN DO

The dead tell the living to live.
—RANE ARROYO

The dead can fly right up to my
window. The dead can be bright
red. The dead can make pictures
come down from walls, and they
can make it so the backyard smells
just like a Christmas tree. The dead

can make a bird land wherever
they want. They can be bright
red if they want. They can make
luck happen, but they can also
make it not. They can curse
your house. They can make

a head of lettuce go bad. They
can wander the streets at night
while I sleep, transmogrify
their tracks sunk in the snow
into those of another mammal.
They can make any song

come on the radio. They can keep
you safe on the road in a whiteout
storm, but they can also not do that.
They can't initiate a rainbow but
if one already comes on the sky
they can add one more.

They hope someone makes
love the way they loved to.
They like visitors at their bones.
Some of them I'm sure
are waiting for their ashes
to be eaten by the young.

egg in space

The shape we make feels like an egg in space, limbs tucked in, a rocking.
A place of possibility and virtuality: emergence and transformation.

—PETRA KUPPERS

BREAKING THE SPELL

Where should I begin about the egg?
Yes, I carried it away in cardboard
(matte package of minor inconveniences)
then drove my gelatinous decoy
into an open area. For plans
as these, which field? Who might
observe my act, knowing in open plains
the curse will be consumed by flames?

I approach the apprehension like a ritual.
Red hot and regular, dead-on and donning
denim for twelve days flat, a ceremony
to unbind all unfortunately hexed
keys while morning the bravest glint
of yolk spreads up behind the salt barn.

STONEWALL SESTINA

Monumental bricks
split open
heroic future
cast in
stone. Pleasure
an angry parade,

loving parade.
Throw bricks
from pleasure
to open
archives in
"better" future.

My future
a parade
receding in
Bustelo bricks,
so open
about pleasure.

Because pleasure
portends future
desire: open.
After parades,
make brick
trafficking in

representation. In
bold pleasure,
my brick

rubs future
clay parades—
I'm open.

Everyone's opening
up in
moans. Dogwood parades
toward pleasure
from future
gravestones.

"Now we've walked in the open," and know that pleasure.
Everything takes place in between sensations and the future
of planets. This queer parade. These blessed stones.

THINGS TO DO IN OLYMPIA

Go look for orange witch's butter growing
     out of dead wood morning after a rain
Take pictures of trees
Measure their trunks with your arms
Drink bubble tea with the miniature
     bubbles from Ding's
Wave to seals from Percival Landing
Visit the piles of wooden poles at the port
Parmesan logs from San Francisco Street Bakery
Roll down your windows on a briny day
Go look for coyote at Nisqually Refuge
Walk around before the fog lifts
Ask the bartender at Brotherhood where to get
     your haircut
Let Tumwater Falls spray the skin of your face
     remember to breathe
Go on a date in Tacoma
Irish coffee at Spar Café in a wooden booth
     where you could, but don't, pull the curtain closed
Clamshells at Tolmie Beach
Giant oak at the Capitol
Wipe gelato from your beard on the boardwalk
Watch salamanders swim at McLane Creek beaver ponds
Salmon teeth washed up along the creek bed
Drink wine and learn about how beavers have sex
Fifteen-dollar Pendletons at Value Village on Sleater Kinney
Greet the mosses
Three-way dates at Swing
     spoons crack crack cracking open the crème brûlée
Bring your notebook around
Dehydrate amanitas and record your dreams

Get a poppy plant for the balcony
Eat an apple
Three slices and a beer from Vic's
Sex with the windows open
Keep Medjool dates on the bedside table
Get rockfish from Olympia Seafood Co.
Cook it into a spicy stew
Look for a rainbow

NOCTURNE

Crepuscular,
I freefall to evening.
Moon that unfurls like a simple mariposa
Marbled & flamboyant seed.
I felt so much pressure to be
Abundant. I plead for something
In green fields extravagant. What
Temples trace mosquitos of this embrace? Sentient filaments, & every strand
Astonished by a canopy
Of decomposing craft, even the cuir lattice. When I want
To cry another noche like a fringe star, I
Pool amorphous beasts
Back into organs. Some temples
Don't feel sinister: "God
Is Change." Me at seventeen
Stitching my wet way
Upstream, arroyo, another
Wrinkle in the gold
Mine. At dawn the veil
Tessellates: LOVE-BRIGHT-LOVE-BRIGHT-LOCK-LILY-OIL.
Even then I kept
Busy with all this traffic . . .
That's why I wander like this.

SUPERNOVA 1987A

The year I was delivered through an incision in my mother's middle because that's the way my sister first came, the news of your collapse reached Earth—an explosion visible to what some called "the unaided eye" and I can't let go of that part. How many rooftop lovers wear glasses, which is a kind of aid? Does my favorite hen lay ejected elements of stars into her yolks?

I think I'd rather wait for your response before I try to figure out what's queer about all this.

ELIZABETH AT THE START

As you all know, tonight
A new volcano has erupted
And now creeps down

Enormous and solid
From a magician's midnight sleeve
We must admire her perfect aim

Moving from left to left, the light
Dawn an unsympathetic yellow
Beneath that loved and celebrated breast

I got up in the night
What's that shining in the leaves
Oh, tree outside my window, we are kin

In your next letter I wish you'd say
Minnow, go to sleep and dream
Instead of gazing at the sea

I am in need of music that would flow
Each day with so much ceremony
The year's doors open

YELLOW IS THE COLOR OF HAPPINESS

Dear Matt
For a long time I wanted to throw eggs at your door
I pictured them smashing
I don't know what I pictured
Walter was not a metaphor
You wanted the eggs without the rooster
You see where I'm going with this
I'm talking about real birds here

I had this idea of flinging the oval wonders at your door
Since you wanted them so bad
I thought about watching them
Crystallize into strange forms
All over your "In this house we believe"
Till the sign looked like a gelatinous Guernica
And the walls came tumbling down

Now let's talk about Walter
Iridescent wings Walter
Did his evolutionary job Walter
Just like the gals
Instinct, he had it
Territory

We are not all Elizabeths—can I *write it?*
Oh hell. Let it be. A disaster.
That some breasts were "loved and celebrated"
Others "horrifying"
And a metaphor flows both ways
Back to the lightbulb one holds and turns in one's hand

GONE IF WE CAN FIGURE OUT WHERE

I don't know why moss grows on this paving stone

       and not

the other ones. Chartreuse. Could be the way eaves

       block

the sun, pouring shade into the window's gullet.

       Why

am I telling you this? I'm chartreuse in the shade.

       Watching

a squirrel drink from pond full of fin rot

       I wonder

what is taste. My aesthetic after all this time is

       I'm still here.

A nervous dehumidifier. You'd never want to drink

       love gathered

like that. Shade rises up in me blocking all the light.

WERKZEUG

Soft, red belly
  of the Cooper's hawk
    pops in bare branches.
      I don't even remember
        thinking of the chickens,

only how sleepy he looked,
  like a tired old man,
    hungry messenger,
      rust-flecked snow.
        Anyway

he won't get the hens now
  the rooster's returned to the yard
    on a permanent basis.
      Walking in woods,
        I said "deer"

and the deer rearranged themselves
  out of the material of trees,
    bark becoming hooves,
      hooves becoming all the ways
        worry had become a weapon

rattling floorboards.
  I wanted the best day of my life.
    Some bright articulation of form
      in landscape. Out of that
        joyful emergency I

knew what love was
    for. Yet I couldn't imagine
    how everything would
        variegate, landscape coming
    back and back.

CONSIDER THE ROOSTER

Who did not ask to join this world any more than I did.
Who scans for trouble as he pecks the ground.
Who announces when a hawk lands in the naked maple above.
Who emits a low trill to warn the flock.
Who does this on instinct to protect potential offspring.
Who rarely takes a treat when offered scrap or seed.
Who instead yips to gather the hens around it.
Who sometimes does this regarding some shiny piece of trash.
Whose wattle catches light the way red lipstick does.
Who slept between breasts as a day-old cockerel.
Whose first attempt to crow sounded like a flopping sock.
Who directs with one stiff wing.
Who we thought would be a hen.
Who reminds all in earshot that like it or not another day has come and gone.
Who disturbs the interior idyll of the neighbor writing lectures on environmental philosophy.
Who keeps the hens alive to lay another day.
Who would risk his life to protect.
Who cockfighters gas up on steroids and provoke to battle.
Who they then point to as an example of how violence is natural among men.
Whose crow can scare away the devil and rouse the dead back to life.
Who will provoke a strong response of either humiliation or joy.

God, I won't be your sacred chicken if it means I have to fight, but I will fight.
I already scan the perimeter.
Testosterone, yes, I take it. Which is not the same as fighting.
The shape you see has nothing to do with me, or the rooster
Who sleeps in a cardboard box in the garage because the philosopher called the police,
Then asked for eggs.
Do you hear that crow that sounds almost like a recording of a crow?
That's daybreak. It is regular like daybreak. Or twilight. It rattles a certain
Window that matches its vibrational frequency. Because the glass, under all that
Strain of air molecules around it, finally decides to change.

alternatives

"If you believe that the vegetation in question does not constitute a public nuisance as outlined above (i.e. an alternative landscape, prairie, garden, etc.) you must file an appeal in writing within *10 days* of the date of this notice."

—THE CITY OF KALAMAZOO, MICHIGAN

WHAT IS A PANDEMIC CHICKEN

Would be a good question except

Everyone already knows. It's hard not to think some god sent a plague among people, but no one asked for this. Now eggs are

expensive and the hens live in Michigan and Olympia and the rooster died, no one's sure why, but Walter Mercado went

       the way of the Jack Gilbert poem where everyone's

       happy the rooster died except the rooster, but nobody

       asks him if he's glad he's gone. Card game at the cidery and chickens come up,

    as a bonding moment between (trans) men.

    Now the music got too slow for me to be able to write. I tell Jenny on the phone I'm trying to figure out

      how to relate to this book now that I left. Pandemic time together and we thought we'd made it,

    thought we were some of the lucky ones. Meanwhile something

sludgy was brewing and during the worst of it, we found out Walter had died, been found dead, and it was like

    when Walter died, we did. The chorus became a coda. Ecstasy element entropy erstwhile example. I remain open open

with some new ways of being closed.

FIELDS THAT I HAVE KNOWN AND LOVED

now that I am becoming disloyal to civilization

now that I move between city and country

now that glyphosate is banned

           now that this is my queer nature

           now that

           now that

                now that I remember the dream

                    now that I remember the sweet smell of each one of you fields

                    like chamomile

                    like the chamomile we plucked for drying

                    in a field that once

                    and as much as I think of a field

as a compositional plane for what C. called

"verbal equinox"

for others it's labor,

"field hands" two

words compounded

two of my favorite words compounded

by the mundane evil of white people

but anyways

as I was saying

what was I saying?

BONE DUST

every part
down to gristle

where meat attaches
to bone—leaves hollow

    having pushed the world away, we call it back through language

                                          love thyself
thy sternum tight like a cage

                        W., R. & T. drop acid and go to a
                        bar inside a grocery store

                              I absorb this information neutrally

                            move toward the scary

        we slipped
    into the crowd escaping. we were first in line to escape. we were trying to fit inside
coolers or buckets, get lifted out

               they mandate
               show us a video
               try to prepare us
               (we are teachers)
               to respond first

               I know I must not be the only

saw it coming and didn't say anything—why?

you should always strive to emit positive vibrations to others, earth, and self

         sun-filled

mouth-breathing
woodpecker
in our bed

                      and I think he is those things

last   living form
on earth

                  (hard to write a poem and let it fail)

what kind of life to not be engaged with desire up to the very end. isn't that what dying is—to no longer be in proximity to want?

                      I wrote, *trees* and non-binary (it was a typo

& a source of positive vibration)

hear flower say no
accept and do not pick it
bringing back the dead

first it was the leg bone. then dark wet owl pellets, fur and bone, tiny skull with bone so fragile it flaked into bone dust, bone soaked in bleach, bone on the back porch, bone of water, bone of light, good boy bone, bone I asked permission for, may I always be ready to hear no: I offer bone as offering, I shake bone around to anyone good who may be listening

what's mine is yours even if it's only bone dust
we live open-hearted and without fear

in the fantasies,
I'm the puppy. I bring back the dead
as a sign of—what?
surrender? having, out in the wilderness,
thought of you?

invoke your
proximate sanctuary, string antidotes together like beads

cat piss — rancher — rearview spider — wasp nest
dead dad blanket for the coldest nights — mountain pass —
antelope — taking a shit under a rainbow in a field of ponies, in Oregon   (how that actually happened)

I know your secret
I too have dropped entire   days into my thigh
nights and galaxies, termites   of testosterone week after
week slow as money even slower when it   crystallizes. I think you are
     beautiful   in me
                         small shocks I did not know I'd   open for

               which is not a secret. sometimes I imagine shapes behind
               my head pouring me into wood chips: me alive, me proximate
               to want, useful as a body for some animal part unashamed by its own rage

               why do you only smell like that after lightning?
               way it sometimes hurts how bad

I close a motionless fist, forget to call you by your other name—

               small pink flag waving in the wind

SETTLER/UNSETTLED

My blood a prophet in a medieval castle with his people—flogged in the streets

                                                                  books burned

                                                                        driven out of town by an angry
                                                        mob

My blood his people who came and built a colony on Buffalo Creek Reservation, believing they had bought it

   that their money ($10.50 per acre plus another $900 for a year of peace) granted them land even though

                                          they had no deed no
                                                          deed no   deed

                                                      & in the house that once sheltered daydreams
                                      for the sawmill operator—

                                                      now a prophet, twenty-four years old, who possessed

   a gift of inspiration—could see and hear, had a scribe
                              for when inspiration struck thereby bridging the gap between idea and the written word, though forking off
the hand-written from the prayer

   Strive for simplicity
   Let yr "yes" be "yes" and "no" be "no"—never take an oath

        & the white men in my blood felled Seneca's trees to build villages—and for all he heard, did not hear "no"?

Actually, yes they left and moved to Iowa.

My Caribbean blood sent kinship through the motherline and some lived

                        open-hearted lay down with many
                              (as I do)

   & women and children lived with women and children, apart from men

      My Spanish blood who came and took Taíno women
                      to lie with
                          "as many as they possibly could," Dr. Chanca wrote

                Conquest for gold
            My blood no immunity

                        O god of chaos—
                        which was he? Doing unto,
                        or done unto him?

           Got settler/unsettled in my blood.

                & Michel and Maria, who fled the boot spur

            to Montreal (where I saw a glorious drag show once, it was so sincere) undocumented to Chicago   no papers   only prayers

Who writes all this down—who remembers?

                                        A coffee bean is actually a seed

                        A deed is a legal instrument
                                meaning evidence
                        I'm out here conjuring someone else's empty stream

                                        for my side

                                                        some knowing when to leave—
                                                        others, removed

But every queer is the family scribe, right?

                                Go back any blood far enough and you'll see a communal kitchen

        Never went to sleep completely—Kept watch—Fished at night—All Night Rituals to be conducted. First order of the
day was ritual bathing and prayers. Morning meal of cassava bread dipped in the communal pepper pot

                                        (I don't bathe every day,
                                                        forget to pray
                                                                eat meals alone have
never planted corn on a hillside during new moon

or carved a canoe from a single tree trunk. Sure I hand-pick through gravel along water's edge—never found gold tho)

                             & the Spanish introduced homophobia to the Taíno—& the Seneca were
made to "move along"—and Billy Graham said AIDS might be God's punishment, & a third of U.S. Americans agreed with him

                                      & women took care of men who were dying

                    & a virus infected the cells, used them as a place to multiply

                                          GRID—"it was never not my battle"

BLOSSOMING OF THE VIOLET AT MIDNIGHT

elemental purpose grows
      fruit from a raspberry beret
           we could all wear them

                lines waking up in me
                 lovers were

                    of this land without

                 being about it
             do you understand
          running low on ways to say it
       and I like sitting in the same corner
    eating the same food watching the same shows
bliss
      and I'm waking up and it's purple here

                              night   fell & got back up again
                and again rolling faster like an engine we had mistakenly built

                  so strong that no one could contain it
                  o life of many melodies

                    o god of rooster song
                  there's something happening in the garden

no, i didn't turn away

BECOMING UPRIGHT AFTER A STRANGE SIESTA

count the altitude
as we climb
further up Jacob's Ladder
it seems to me now
like a dream

a strange rotation
revelations

sitting
across a mesa
where once I saw green
(moss) now it is red (clay)
breathe

out walking in Rocky : Dad announces
we're a mile and a half above Olympia

walking

the metal on the car covered in the dust of red rocks

NEW MOON NEWTON

stars
whole patterns of them
rocking around in the radiant arena
above and around our heads
on a night when the wind
sang like a scream
and the deer stood frozen
as a statue of itself
the sky was dark because
la luna had finished revealing themself
and was not yet ready to
begin again

and I get it now:
a stanza is like a little frame

and the frame is a little crooked

jenny
calls from the road and we talk
I walk
so briefly we together
move from our faraway states
synced perhaps by the clap
of hooves and burning oil
and the telephone can be a line
like any other wire

so can I say it:
love frightens me
the matter it contains

the speed the direction
even words of thanks
at the reference desk
from a patron
gracias, amor
haunt me in the quiet places . . .

but if "god is change"
then is it god who sent my matter
hurtling back into the open open

can anybody tell me how to contain it

clockwork
even the moon
on a calendar stacked
fluxes away and comes back

striking disclosure
arrives in flashes

FIRST LIGHT

Both times leaving Boise
    when still the eyes of animals
        along some blackened road

matched the stars still
    climbing the celestial dome
and we drove east toward

        sunup as day became
        another day right

        there in front of our eyes. I was with
family men and the mountain

        was never the point until
            everything laid bare as if

        focused by headlights into
            coyote crossing one realm
into another while we snaked

up to elevation trying once
        again for higher ground but
            trying different this time.

DUSK IS AN EXAMPLE

making a time

& place from

in-between

at dusk the pines

so still they

look fake,

arms outstretched

unflappable against

dimming of the light

unflappable against
dimming of the light

what's so bad about
darkness anyway?

aside from visions
it brings out

carousel
coming to life inside
your very eyes

nighttime is happiness
(or it could be)

not one motion giving
them up as the living

living things they are

total stillness
on every side

the way at dusk I'm
glued
to windows

scanning snow for tracks

proof of life amid
diabolical wind drift

solitude that awaits

every one of us inside a

treehouse,
                              each time

like the very first time

would you come away
with me?

before night falls?

astonished at the years

available to us so far

I had to stop and
listen to the music
for a moment there

still evergreens refuse

to let down their hair

one part of me stayed
up all night writing

another part of me slept

following a red fox toward

switchbacks of my

life. these years

these days and

                    moments

the trees held sentry

          solemn all night

like a holiday or

hibernation

and it was that

and it was that

NO, I DIDN'T TURN AWAY FROM THE WITCH'S BUTTER . . .

or the walks . . . or the briny sea . . . all the mosses . . .
middays with R . . . I remember you . . . it's this . . . orange . . .
fungus that emerges after rain . . . teaching me . . .
that everything goes away . . . and opens . . . in certain conditions . . .
open . . . close . . . open . . . close . . .
a witch passed through here in the night,
so the story goes. (volta breathe.)
that's all I'm doing, is moving closer to my life.

Lynda says stay, stay behind the story
and a walk can be a poem like any other path (breathe).
close . . . open . . . close . . . open . . . close . . . open . . .
all form follows song through an open space.
so no, if you ask me, did I turn away,
but I did, but I did turn towards myself.

ELEGY FOR WALTER, FROM THE FUTURE

No more Michigan, no more Washington,
what rattled in my ribcage still awakens me.
No more gals in the backyard bossed
by a miniature piñata with pretty wings.
No more teardrop, no more rabbits,
hope these gone pieces of my life

are together somewhere out there. Is it true
you died so I could live?
Or is there no scheming rhyme?
Some leaves fall and other ones
don't, whim of the wind.

And who'd go back to Michigan?
That place was early death for me,
I've learned
some have to choose over and over to live,
and some of us do.

I think if you were here you'd get it.

Laying there
next to my
stockpile, hearing what sounded like
you practicing your crow and it was: the civil disturbance
that rattled my skedaddle out of there. Walter.

Another near miss.
I knew all along, had seen
inside my dream: the letters of your crow jumble, become
an arc, dissolving into rain, or confetti—

an invitation I accepted through intense and sudden
connections with whatever your frequency shattered.
I rode your rainbow rainbow all the way to

high desert, and even here,
I remember,
morning now so unannounced.

TRANSIT

Back to the page, which welcomes

as a wild field welcomes   wildly.
Stars above, do they move too?
"Death takes care of all."

Words moving according to melody,
in other words, music.

Walk through the middle of the trail even
when it's muddy.

I left

I lived

Coyote
crossed in front

Wondering if or
when I'd be back

Now I'm flying through the air
        propelled by
love of family and friends.

I sing as loud as I can in the car
        and it's pleasure.

Maybe that's why Matt hated
      the rooster and wouldn't let it go.

Because you can't hear its crow
      and stay the same.

What's next?
I'll visit New Mexico.

                Look, I'm singing.

                That's where Walter lives now.

                Bless me, Walter, before you really go.

Good morning to all,
      and to all a safe passage.

Someone says "See you around"
      and I experience this as
      a concrete image.

          Yes, meet you on the circle.

Meet you on the loop.

You'll meet what I mean soon.

I've got to go, I've been asked
        to deliver a lecture
        and there are so many words to retrieve . . .

Dear Caelan, I'm far from shore.
No witch's butter here
But in the lichen and moss sprouting
as miracles on craggy
rockface, I see those
woods in miniature, my whole year
and more stretching out. Until I'm
so far zoomed out that everything
is beautiful again. Not despite. Look around.
Every day is a blue sky, I'm
so much closer to the sun.

The wind with its wild arms pulls
my car to the side of the lane on
the diagonal.

Yes, something's brewing.
Something is dawning.

CLAIRVOYANCE

Some god drew eyes all over
the trunks of aspen, and then,
on account of godlike things, began,
from some eyes, to grow new
limbs out of the pupils,
out into the open
of the windy atmosphere. *What have you seen?*
I wondered of the aspen, and do they
wonder the same of me? And
you reading this, what have you known?
The moon, almost full, rising in a pale
blue sky?

I prefer to listen, looking one way,
then the other.
I look at mouths when they speak.
I like to look at what you look at.
Maybe I am looking for a future,
word after sequential word
strung together to make an image.
The way my dad,
through binoculars, looks.
Not scrutiny, but something else.
Everywhere I look, eyes. Ocular
patterns on the aspen.
I have seen the future:
something begins to sprout,
making contact—

NOTES

THE EPIGRAPHS:

The poem "Roosters" by Elizabeth Bishop.

The poem "Cuba, 1962" by Ai.

Poem #215 by Emily Dickinson.

"23. NorthPrairieCity" from Critical Poly 100's by Dr. Kim TallBear.

Close to the Knives: A Memoir of Disintegration by David Wojnarowicz.

"Wild Heart" by Stevie Nicks.

"Writing With the Salamander: An Ecopoetic Community Performance Project" by Petra Kuppers.

THE POEMS:

"I Just Chose My Place and Let the Circle Form Around Me": The italicized portions of this poem together comprise a passage from the book *Amana That Was and Amana That Is* by Bertha Shambaugh (published in 1932 by The State Historical Society of Iowa).

"Ram's Head White Hollyhock and Little Hills": Georgia O'Keeffe's painting by a similar name.

"God of Medicine": The account of Socrates' final hours comes to us from Plato's long dialogue *Phaedo*. In his article "The Mystery of Socrates' Last Words," Colin Wells wrote that "Asclepius was the Greek god of healing, and offering a cock in sacrifice was a way of thanking him for healing Socrates with the hemlock."

"Offerings Iphis Pledged as a Girl and Paid as a Boy": The title is a phrase from Ovid's *Metamorphoses* (Bk 9, ln 794 Penguin Classics edition).

"Michigan": Sylvia Rivera's speech, now known as "Y'all Better Quiet Down," which she gave on June 24, 1973, during the Christopher Street Liberation Day Rally in Washington Square Park, NYC. About the "x' in the third-to-last-line of this poem, see Alan Pelaez Lopez's essay "The X In Latinx Is A Wound, Not A Trend," in *ColorBloq*.

"Frequently the Woods are Pink": See Emily Dickinson's poem by the same title.

"Rx": The poem "Dear Shorty (No. 6)" by Willie Perdomo.

"Expanding the Encounter": The last three lines are from a poem by Rumi, translated by Coleman Barks, called "The Diver's Clothes." See Barry Lopez's essay "The Invitation," from *Embrace Fearlessly the Burning World*."

"Stonewall Sestina": The phrase "Now we've walked in the open" is from Dick Leitsch's 1969 account of the Stonewall uprising, published in *The Gay View*, the newsletter of the Mattachine Society. He was the first gay reporter to document the events at Stonewall.

"What the Dead Can Do": See Rane Arroyo's essay "Introduction: Some Debts Are Angels," from *The Buried Sea: New and Selected Poems*.

"Nocturne": Began in Brenda Cárdenas's CantoMundo workshop. Its line "god is change" references Octavia E. Butler's *Parable of the Sower*.

"Elizabeth at the Start": This poem is composed of first lines from Elizabeth Bishop poems.

"What is a pandemic chicken": See the poem "The Rooster," by Jack Gilbert.

"Settler/Unsettled": Dr. Chanca refers to Diego Álvarez Chanca, a physician who accompanied

Christopher Columbus on his second colonizing expedition west, to the Caribbean, from 1493–1494. The phrase "the gift of inspiration" refers to the Community of True Inspiration, or Inspirationists, a religious group from 1714–1932 that decided after facing persecution in Germany to seek religious freedom in the United States, and settled a communal life in the Amana Colonies in Iowa. They were one of the longest-lasting communal societies in the United States. My paternal grandfather was an elder in the church. Certain members were called by God to serve as Werkzeuge, or instruments, who delivered awakenings orally. More information can be found at inspirationistarchive.org. "GRID" was an early name for HIV: "gay-related immune deficiency." "It was never not my battle" was said by ACT UP veteran Alexis Danzig ("The Women Who Fought AIDS," *Vice*.)

"New Moon Newton": Butler, *Parable of the Sower*.

ACKNOWLEDGMENTS

Academy of American Poets' *Poem-a-Day*: "New Moon Newton"

American Poetry Review: "Becoming Particulate" and "Elizabeth at the Start"

The Best American Poetry 2022: "What the Dead Can Do"

Black Warrior Review: "I Want Biodegradable Sex," "Who Profits From This Feeling," and "Ram's Head White Hollyhock and Little Hills"

BOMB: "Settler/Unsettled"

The Carolina Quarterly: "Colony Collapse"

The Cincinnati Review: "Impervious"

Denver Quarterly: "Nocturne"

ISLE: Interdisciplinary Studies in Literature and Environment: "Michigan" and "Rx"

The Nation: "I Just Chose My Place and Let the Circle Form Around Me"

New England Review: "Consider the Rooster," "Werkzeug," "Offerings Iphis Pledged as a Girl and Paid as a Boy," and "Everyone Wants Some of My Prairie"

Orion: "All I Have is the Woods Inside My Head"

Oversound: "Boreal"

Poetry Daily: "I Want Biodegradable Sex" (reprint)

POETRY Magazine: "Bone Dust" and "T4T"

The Rumpus: "Will and Testament"

The Yale Review: "Everything All at Once" and "Clairvoyance"

West Branch: "Stonewall Sestina" and "What the Dead Can Do"

With deepest gratitude to—

National Endowment for the Arts, for the time and support to write.

The entire team at Nightboat Books: Stephen Motika, Lindsey Boldt, Lina Bergamini, Kit Schluter, Dante Silva, Emily Bark Brown, Santiago Valencia, Kazim Ali. It has been an honor collaborating with you to bring this book into print. I am grateful for your vision, support, humor, care, creativity, and understanding. You make it easy to be proud to be with the press.

Caelan Nardone, this book's editor, for your encouragement and conversations through manuscript revisions, and for believing in the possibilities. Your belief is all over these pages.

Helen Armstrong-Weier, my literary assistant, for your indispensable support on this journey.

National Endowment for the Arts, for the time and space to write.

Each person who invited me to teach/speak in your programs as I worked on this book, especially at: The MFA Program at Warren Wilson College, University of British Columbia, Fine Arts Work Center, Bread Loaf Environmental Writers' Conference, Vermont Studio Center.

CantoMundo poetas, for our summer of teach-ins and solidarity out of which this book began.

Friends, Confidantes, Pen Pals, Readers, Loves: Aerik Francis, Alex Smith, Allison Crowley, Andrea Lawlor, Angeline Shaka, Brian Teare, CAConrad, Carolyn Wine, Cate Barry, Chelsea Reimann, Ching-In Chen, Desmond Rhodes-Chang, Evan Rhodes, Gabrielle Calvocoressi, Hank Rhodes-Chang, James in Olympia, Jennifer Chang, Jenny Johnson, Jeremy Hilgert, KC Councilor, Leah Lakshmi Piepzna-Samarasinha, Lucas de Lima, Margaret Rhee, Marwa Helal, Maya Marshall, Meg Day, Rana in Olympia, Samuel Ace, Suzanne Gold, Temim Fruchter, Wo Chan.

Dr. Joshua Gilens and Gio Rubio: I am grateful for your care and healing.

Analiese Baez Brown, my amazing sister: I love you. We got this. Thank you for everything—you've been my rock.

Jason Brown, for your profound support and unwavering presence.

My parents, their parents, theirs, and so on. Many cousins. And those who've come before us, and gone before us, too.

To my coven.

Special appreciation to my teachers and my students.

My trans kin.

And Claude, Dilly, Walter, Owly, Sylvia, Frida Eugene, Sisters, Florence, Amy, and Rainbow: "May you bloom and grow / bloom and grow forever." —Edelweiss

AUTHOR PORTRAIT BY JENNIFER KOSKINEN

OLIVER BAEZ BENDORF is the author of two previous collections of poems: *Advantages of Being Evergreen* (2019) and *The Spectral Wilderness* (2015). He has received fellowships and awards from the National Endowment for the Arts, The Publishing Triangle, Canto-Mundo, Lambda Literary, Vermont Studio Center, and the Wisconsin Institute for Creative Writing. He teaches in the low-residency MFA Program for Writers at Warren Wilson College. Born and raised in Iowa, he now lives along the Front Range of the Rocky Mountains, in Colorado.

NIGHTBOAT BOOKS

Nightboat Books, a nonprofit organization, seeks to develop audiences for writers whose work resists convention and transcends boundaries. We publish books rich with poignancy, intelligence, and risk. Please visit nightboat.org to learn about our titles and how you can support our future publications.

The following individuals have supported the publication of this book. We thank them for their generosity and commitment to the mission of Nightboat Books:

Kazim Ali, Anonymous (5), Ava Avnisan, Jean C. Ballantyne, Bill Bruns, V. Shannon Clyne, The Estate of Ulla Dydo, Photios Giovanis, Amanda Greenberger, David Groff, Parag Rajendra Khandhar, Vandana Khanna, Shari Leinwand, Johanna Li, Elizabeth Madans, Martha Melvoin, Care Motika, Elizabeth Motika, The Leslie Scalapino – O Books Fund, Amy Scholder, Thomas Shardlow, Ira Silverberg, Benjamin Taylor, Jerrie Whitfield and Richard Motika, and Issam Zineh

This book is made possible, in part, by grants from the New York City Department of Cultural Affairs in partnership with the City Council, the National Endowment for the Arts, and the New York State Council on the Arts Literature Program.